LEARN TO DRAW

Disney

Classic
Animated Movies
Volume 1

Walter Foster
Jr.

This library edition published in 2017 by Walter Foster Jr.,
an imprint of Quarto Publishing Group USA Inc.
6 Orchard Road, Suite 100
Lake Forest, CA 92630

The Aristocats is based on the book by Thomas Rowe.
Illustrated by the Disney Storybook Artists

Distributed in the United States and Canada by
Lerner Publisher Services
241 First Avenue North
Minneapolis, MN 55401 U.S.A.
www.lernerbooks.com

First Library Edition

Library of Congress Cataloging-in-Publication Data

Names: Disney Storybook Artists, illustrator.
Title: Learn to draw Disney's classic animated movies / illustrated by the
   Disney Storybook Artists.
Description: Library [edition]. | Lake Forest, CA : Walter Foster Jr., 2017.
Identifiers: LCCN 2016032740| ISBN 9781942875192 (v. 1 : hardcover) | ISBN
   9781942875208 (v. 2 : hardcover)
Subjects: LCSH: Drawing--Technique--Juvenile literature. | Cartoon
   characters--Juvenile literature.
Classification: LCC NC1764 .L3453 2017 | DDC 741.5/8--dc23
LC record available at https://lccn.loc.gov/2016032740

Printed in USA
9 8 7 6 5 4 3 2 1

Table of Contents

Tools and Materials

You only need to gather a few simple art supplies before you begin. Start with a drawing pencil and an eraser. Make sure you also have a pencil sharpener and a ruler. To add color to your drawings, use markers, colored pencils, crayons, watercolors, or acrylic paint. The choice is yours!

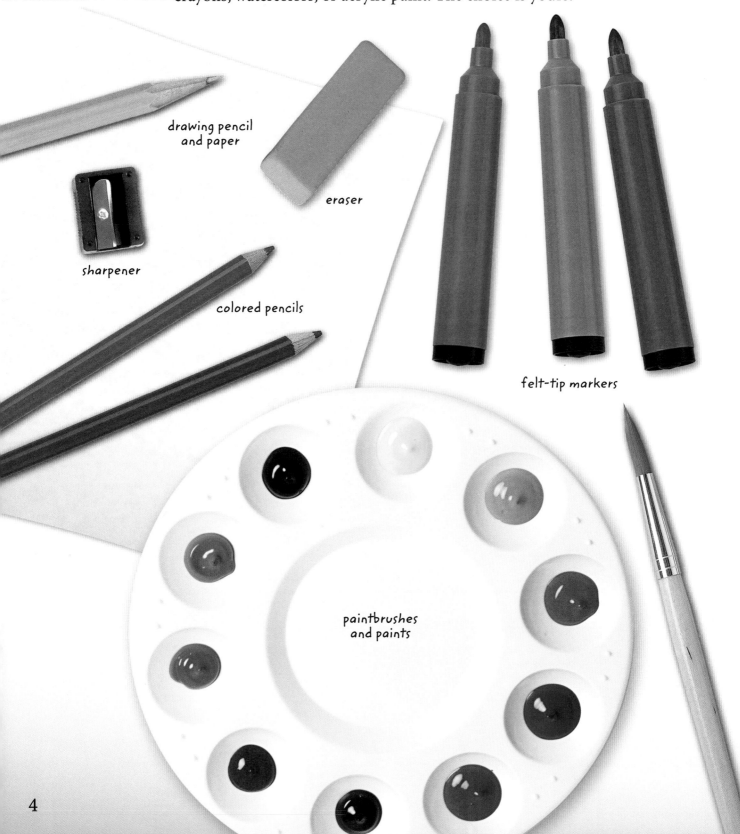

drawing pencil and paper

eraser

sharpener

colored pencils

felt-tip markers

paintbrushes and paints

How to Use This Book

You can draw any of the characters in this book by following these simple steps.

First draw the basic shapes, using light lines that will be easy to erase.

Each new step is shown in blue, so you'll always know what to draw next.

Take your time and copy the blue lines, adding detail.

Darken the lines you want to keep, and erase the rest.

Add color to your drawing with colored pencils, markers, paints, or crayons!

PETER PAN

The self-assured and childish Peter Pan lives in Never Land, where no one ever has to grow up. For Peter, life is one big adventure, and he spends his days fighting pirates and handing out orders to his crew of Lost Boys. He likes stories, especially ones about himself, and he always wears a red feather on the left side of his cap.

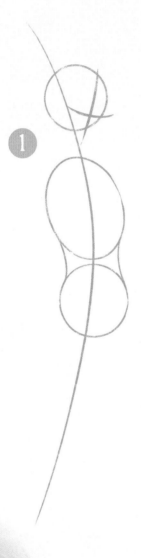

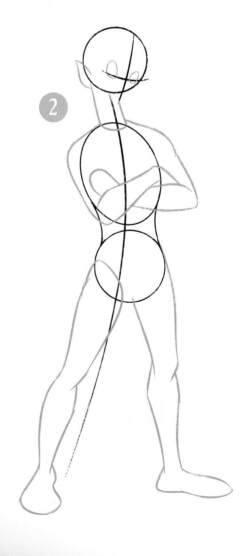

6

③

6

THE DARLING CHILDREN

Wendy Darling's bedtime stories about the heroic Peter Pan
fascinate her younger brothers, John and Michael. When Peter
overhears their father's plan to move Wendy out of the nursery,
he offers to take the Darling children back to Never Land with him, where
the stories never have to end and the children never have to grow up.

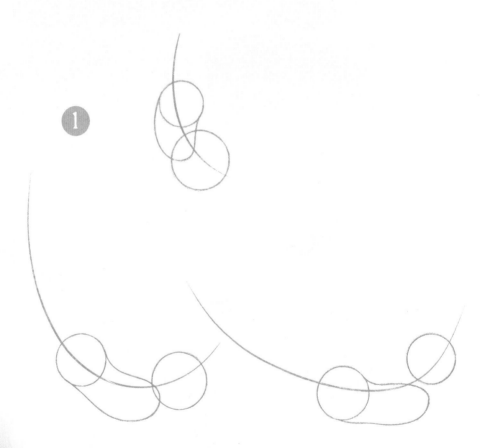

6

TINKER BELL

Tinker Bell is a loyal and overprotective fairy
friend of Peter Pan. Wherever she goes, a trail of pixie
dust follows, and her voice sounds like the tinkling of tiny bells.
Tinker Bell's rounded pixie look is carried from the balls on the
tips of her toes to the little bun on top of her head.

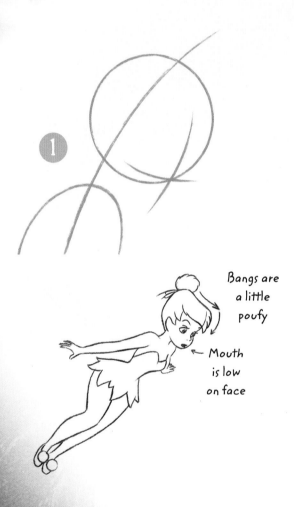

Bangs are
a little
poufy

Mouth
is low
on face

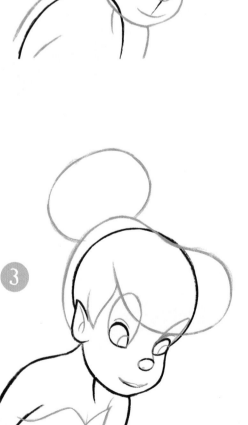

YES! flat on top

NO! not round

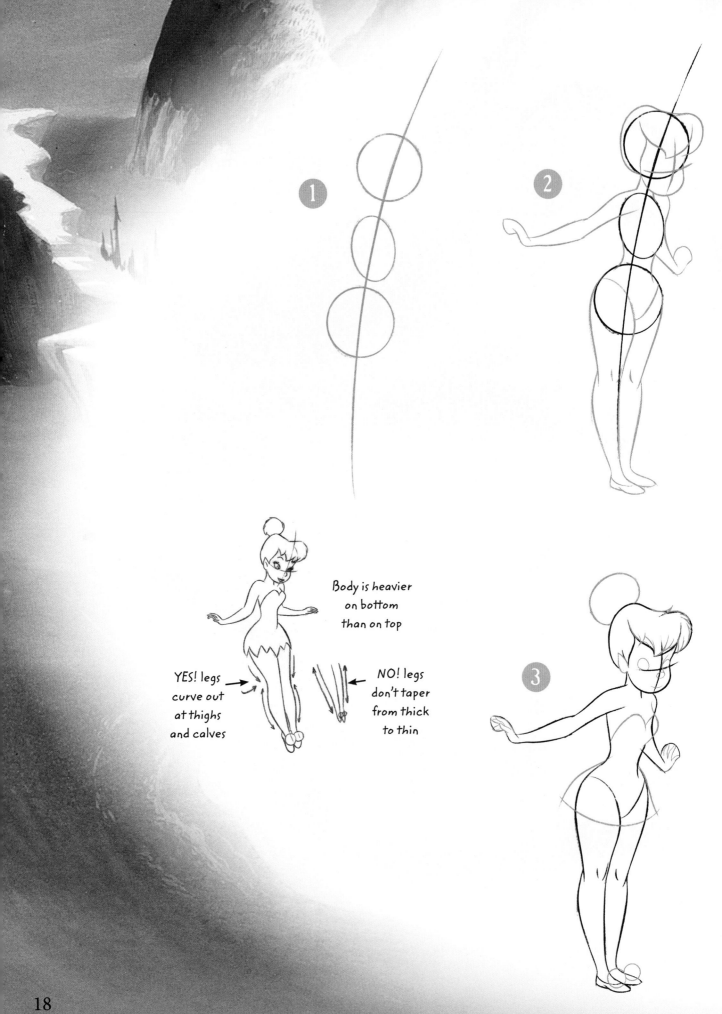

Body is heavier
on bottom
than on top

YES! legs
curve out
at thighs
and calves

NO! legs
don't taper
from thick
to thin

4

Skirt is short
and flares a bit
at bottom

YES! ragged
bottom edge

NO! not
even shapes

5

6

19

CAPTAIN HOOK

Captain Hook is no longer sailing the seven seas searching for treasure. Instead, he's hunting down Peter Pan, and he won't stop until he has his revenge! Although he lost his hand years ago to the tick-tock crock that follows him wherever he sails, Captain Hook remains a skilled swordsman, ready to duel with Peter every chance he gets.

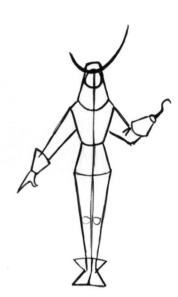

Captain Hook is tall and thin with a hook on his left hand

Shape of hat is uneven;
the plume comes out
of the center crown

5

6

Moustache is
symmetrical with
very long ends

MR. SMEE

The bumbling and thick-skinned Mr. Smee is Captain Hook's right-hand man and first mate. He's a portly fellow, who can always be found wearing half-moon glasses and a bright red stocking cap. Mr. Smee is loyal to a fault. Even though he longs to leave Never Land and return to the open sea, he follows his captain's villainous orders wherever they may take him.

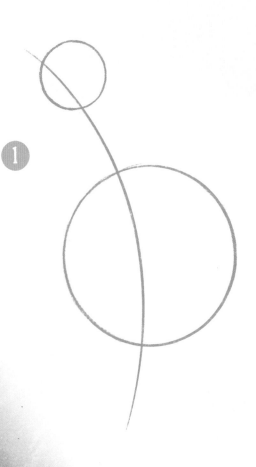

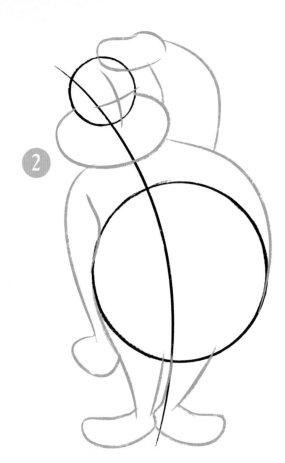

6

Bambi

Young Bambi is a shy and curious deer who lives with his mother in the forest and plays with his best friends, Thumper, a bunny, and Flower, a skunk. Bambi wobbles with youthful exuberance on his four slender legs, and his small muzzle and wide eyes allow artists to create a variety of realistic, childlike expressions.

1

2

3

4

5

6

29

Thumper

Young Thumper is a loud bunny who likes to eat blossoms and give his forest friends plenty of advice. He has a full, fluffy chest and oversized feet, and he is made up of soft, curving lines. Like a real rabbit, Thumper uses his large hind feet to spring into action.

4

5

6

Pinocchio

The wooden puppet, Pinocchio, is brought to life by the Blue Fairy one night after his creator, Geppetto, wishes upon a star for a child. Although he has a loving father and a "conscience" in a trustworthy cricket named Jiminy, he still struggles to make sense of right and wrong. If he can be brave and learn to be truthful, he stands a chance of becoming a real boy.

Geppetto

The lonely woodcarver, Geppetto, lives with his fashionable fish, Cleo, and his spoiled kitten, Figaro, but he dreams of having a son. The Blue Fairy hears his wish and rewards Geppetto for his generous heart by bringing to life his latest creation, a puppet named Pinocchio. When Pinocchio goes missing, Geppetto is relentless in his search to bring him home safely, even taking on the fierce whale, Monstro.

Jiminy Cricket

Jiminy Cricket, or "Lord High Keeper of the Knowledge of Right and Wrong, Counselor in Moments of Temptation, and Guide along the Straight and Narrow Path," as the Blue Fairy has appointed him, is a humble and wise cricket who can carry a whistling tune. Though his advice isn't always heeded, he tries to help Pinocchio stay true on his journey to become a real boy—and he looks rather spiffy doing it with his new spats, top hat, and umbrella.

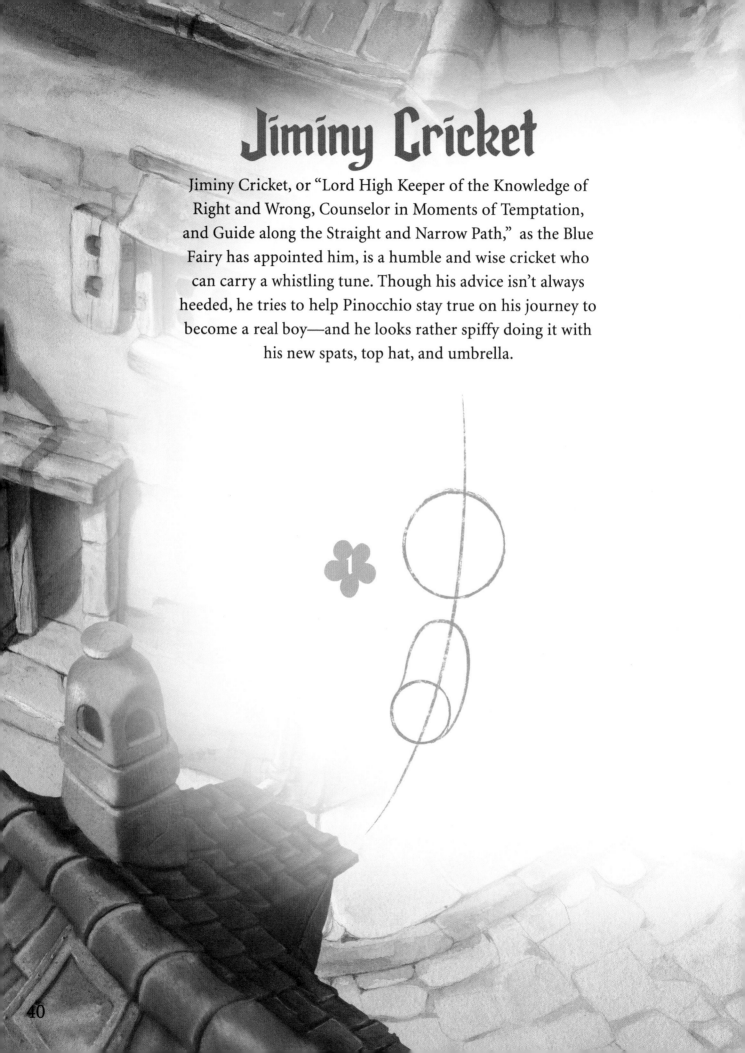

6

Lady

Lady is a privileged cocker spaniel with soulful brown eyes, and she absolutely adores Jim Dear and Darling, her owners. Left in the care of Aunt Sarah while the two go on vacation, Lady is unfairly muzzled and runs away from home. When a pack of street dogs corners her, Tramp comes to her rescue, sparking a love story for the ages.

Tramp

A mutt from the wrong side of the tracks, Tramp falls head over heels for Lady, or "Pidge," as he calls her. He roams the streets without a collar, always one step ahead of the dogcatcher. To Tramp, the world is his dog bowl, and he does his best to show Lady that life can be a bit thrilling and fun once you're off the leash.

Si and Am

This destructive duo is always looking to cause trouble. Si and Am are Aunt Sarah's sneaky twin Siamese cats who love to get into mischief and let others, in this case Lady, take the blame. Don't forget to include their crooked tails and exposed teeth.

Note the angle for the placement of the eyes, which will help create their expressions

Si and Am have three whiskers
on each side of the face

Thomas O'Malley

Thomas O'Malley, or Abraham DeLacey Giuseppe Casey Thomas O'Malley the alley cat, is an orange tabby with a free spirit and devil-may-care attitude. But that all changes (mostly), when he meets Duchess, a well-bred beauty whom he falls in love with at first sight.

Duchess

The ever-classy Duchess is a white Persian cat who lives with her three kittens, Marie, Berlioz, and Toulouse, and the wealthy Madame Bonfamille in Paris. But when Edgar, the Madame's faithful butler, catches whiff of his boss's plan to change her will and leave everything to her cats, he dumps her beloved animals somewhere in the countryside. Frightened and left to fend for themselves, Duchess and her kittens meet Thomas O'Malley, a jazzy cat who helps them make their way back to the city.

Marie

Marie takes after her mother and always wears a pretty pink bow between her ears. She's constantly tattling on her brothers and getting them into trouble. When the three kittens fight, Marie can be rather sassy, sticking out her tongue and forgetting to be the lady that she is. But unlike her brothers, Marie's a romantic, and she finds Mr. O'Malley to be absolutely dreamy.

SORCERER'S APPRENTICE MICKEY

Mickey is apprentice to the mighty sorcerer, Yen Sid. Though his daily life is filled with magic, Mickey's duties revolve around humdrum chores, such as carrying buckets of water from a nearby well. One night, when Yen Sid goes off to bed, Mickey steals his magical hat and uses his power to cast a spell that will finally allow him some rest—or so he thinks.

When the tops of Mickey's
hands show, be sure to add the
stitching lines to his gloves!

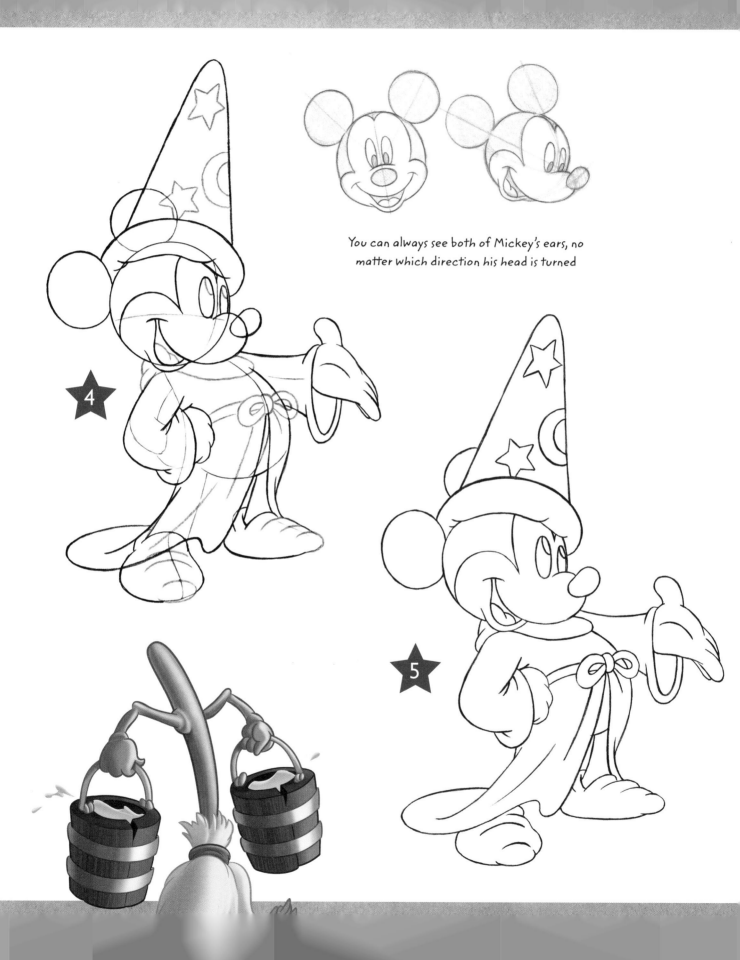

You can always see both of Mickey's ears, no matter which direction his head is turned

Mickey's eyebrows can
show how he's feeling

YEN SID

The powerful sorcerer Yen Sid spends most of his time in his tower, casting spells and mastering his abilities. When his untrained apprentice gets ahold of his sorcerer's hat and turns the tower into a watery mess, Yen Sid must come to the rescue and set things right again.

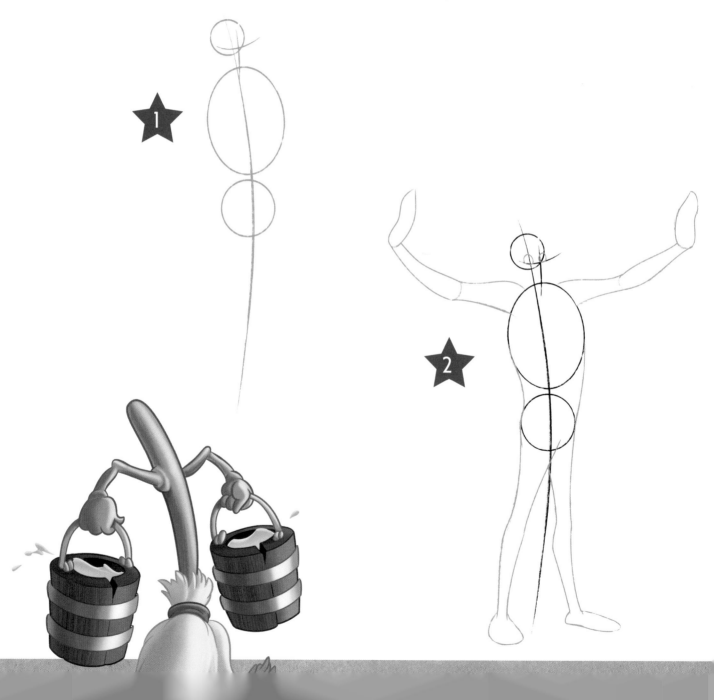

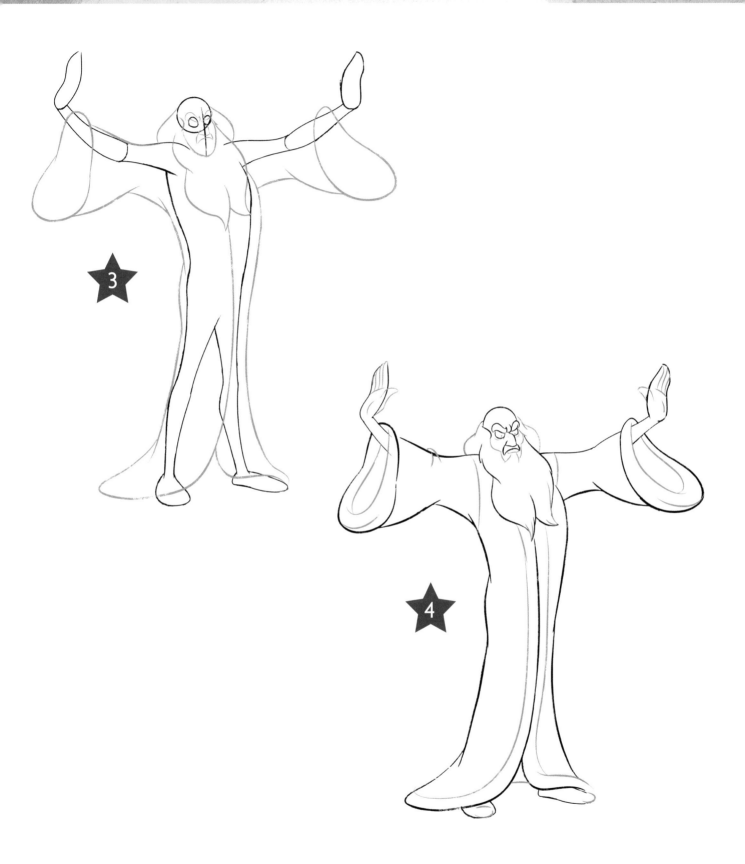

The End